Mike Keneally

Illustrated by Peter Ferguson

STECK-VAUGHN

Harcourt Supplemental Publishers

www.steck-vaughn.com

Cover illustration by Peter Scanlan

ISBN 0-7398-7525-6

Printed in China.

1 2 3 4 5 6 7 8 9 M 07 06 05 04 03

Contents

CHAPTER 1
No Time for Fun

"Can you please quiet down, honey?" Thayla's mom asked, walking into the living room. "Don't you have homework to do?"

"I have to practice, Mom!" said Thayla.

Thayla Groono loved to practice her music gloves. The more she waved her gloves, the more they glowed with color. As she waved them, they pumped beautiful music into the air. Thayla's years of study with Bombo, the city's music teacher, were paying off.

Her mom was in no mood to listen to the music, though. It was Saturday morning, and she had just come home from work.

Mrs. Groono made machine parts in a factory. She had been working almost every night for weeks. The factory workers didn't get many breaks, and Mrs. Groono was always tired when she came home.

Thayla's family and others like them were called Insiders. The Insiders lived in a city on the planet Landor. The city was covered by a giant dome that kept out Landor's harsh and stormy weather. At least that's what the city's factory owners had always told the Insiders.

"Did you have a rough night, dear?" asked Mr. Groono as his wife walked into the small kitchen. He was eating a bowl of gray mush. All the Insiders ate mush for breakfast.

"I sure did," Mrs. Groono sighed. She threw an envelope onto the table. "You'll never believe what they did," she said, taking off her jacket.

Mr. Groono turned the envelope upside down. Computer chips fell out. On Landor, computer chips were used for money.

"There's one less chip than last week!" said Mr. Groono.

"That's right," said Thayla's mom. "The factory owners keep cutting our pay, and the store owners keep raising the price of food. How is our family supposed to have a good life this way?"

"Bombo says that playing music is the key to happiness for all Insiders!" Thayla called from the living room.

"My music teacher told me the same thing when I was young," said Mr. Groono, rolling his eyes. "Music is fun when you're a kid, but it won't help us in the real world. Business just hasn't been good lately. Workers are getting pay cuts at my factory, too."

Mrs. Groono narrowed her eyes. "If times are so tough, then why are the factory owners building such big homes? I can see their fancy new furniture right through their windows."

"Well, you know we're lucky compared to our neighbors Outside," said Mr. Groono. "We all have jobs, houses, and clothes. The poor Outsiders can't say the same."

"Yes, you're right," sighed Mrs. Groono. "I forgot about the Outsiders."

The Outsiders lived outside the dome. The Insiders made machine parts for them, and in return, Outsiders sold machines, games, and movies to the Insiders.

Insiders were not allowed to go outside the dome walls. The factory owners were also the city leaders, and they were always telling the Insiders that Outsiders had tough lives. The owners said that there was a lot of crime Outside. They said that Outsiders were poor and often stole things from each other. Harsh, stormy weather on Landor was another reason why Insiders were not allowed to leave their dome. Only the factory owners and the guards at the dome's gates had ever seen Outsiders or been Outside.

Mrs. Groono was too tired to be angry anymore. She sat down in the living room and watched the tele-visor. The tele-visor played movies brought in from Outside. It was also a special kind of TV that you could talk into. People shown on the tele-visor could see and talk to anyone watching them, too.

The tele-visor was showing a message from the factory owners. "Today is Saturday," the message read. "The weather is nice, thanks to the dome. Have a safe day!"

Mr. Groono joined his wife on the couch. "Come sit with us, Thayla," he said.

"No, thanks. I'm going to meet Rando," replied Thayla.

Thayla put her music gloves in her pocket. She looked sadly at her parents on the couch. They were always too tired for anything but watching the tele-visor. She wondered if she would be like them someday. *I'd better have fun now, while I'm still young*, she thought.

"I'll be back soon—I promise!" said Thayla as she ran out the door. ♪

During the day, Insiders could always see the milky-gray dome around their city. They couldn't see through it, though. It was made of ice four feet thick. The ice was held in place and kept frozen by a special force field.

Thayla walked with her friend, Rando Nann, to the dome's main gates. Rando loved watching the flying trucks float through the gates, carrying machine parts Outside. As the two friends walked, Rando played with a special camera called a snap-shooter. He had borrowed it from school for a project.

"Check out what this thing can do!" he said. He pointed the snap-shooter at a tree and clicked a button. A snapshot popped up on a small screen at the back of the camera. The picture showed what was beside and in front of the tree. Rando clicked another button, and the picture showed what was behind the tree.

"I don't know why people say Outsiders are so unhappy compared to us," Rando said. "I'd be happy if I could build things like this."

"Point it at the flying trucks," Thayla said.

"Great idea!" Rando replied. He ran off.

"Wait!" Thayla cried. "I didn't mean it. We're not allowed near the trucks!"

It was too late. Rando ran over to a spot where workers were placing boxes from the factories onto the ground. Guards stood by, watching closely. A robot hand came out from the roof of a nearby truck. It quickly grabbed a box from the ground and put it in the cargo space at the back of the truck.

Thayla ran over to Rando. "The guards will see us!" she whispered.

"No, they won't," he said. "They're looking away now. Come on!"

Rando jumped out from behind a tree and pointed his snap-shooter at a truck. Before he knew what was happening—*ka-poomf!*—the truck's robot hand had reached out, grabbed him, and tossed him into the cargo space.

Thayla ran over to help Rando, but all of a sudden—*ka-poomf!*—the robot hand grabbed her, too. In a moment, she was lying in the back of the truck with Rando.

Rando and Thayla sat up and looked at each other. Things had happened so quickly that the two friends didn't know what to do next. As they caught their breath, they heard voices outside the truck.

"That's the last box!" someone shouted.

The robot hand shut the truck's back doors, and the truck sped away. Thayla and Rando bounced around inside. Then they heard a dome gate opening.

"Oh, no!" cried Thayla. "I think the truck is taking us Outside!"

CHAPTER 2

Inside the Outside World

As the truck sped along, Rando peeked out of a window on the back door. He frowned and put his hand over his eyes. "What is that bright light?"

"I think it's sunlight," said Thayla. "You'd better get away from that window. Remember what the factory owners are always telling us? Sunlight will burn your skin."

"It's hard to believe that," said Rando. "Sunlight feels kind of nice."

Rando leaned against the window for more light. Suddenly the truck stopped. Its back door popped open, and Rando fell out.

Thayla tried to catch him. Instead, she found herself tumbling out of the truck with Rando. Luckily for them, the truck was floating just a few inches above the ground.

Thayla and Rando found themselves in an alley behind a store. Robot hands were putting boxes from the truck onto a belt that led into the store. The young Insiders hid quickly.

Minutes later, the flying truck was on its way to another store. Rando and Thayla watched as it sped away. They couldn't quite believe what was happening.

"I think we're on our own," Thayla said, her voice shaking a bit. ⚡

Slowly the two friends walked to the end of the alley and peeked around the corner. There they saw an amazing sight. They were in the center of an Outsider city! Shops and trees lined a wide street. Moms and dads walked with their kids and their pets. A few people sold ice cream. Flying cars zipped past the two Insiders. Everyone wore colorful clothes, and no one wore a work suit. ⚡

The only time Thayla had seen such bright colors was when she put on her music gloves. Her hands searched for them in her pockets. She pulled them on and felt them tingle as they warmed up. Then she and Rando headed down the street.

It's so beautiful, Thayla thought. Back home under the dome, the sky was always gray. The clothes were gray. The food was gray. Even the leaves on the trees looked gray.

Thayla's heart soared as she and Rando wandered through the streets of the city. She looked at the horizon for factory chimneys, but she didn't see any.

Many people in the Outsiders' city sat in parks playing games. Thayla saw a family having a picnic on a patch of grass. She sat under a tree and leaned over to smell some flowers. She couldn't believe how sweet and wonderful they smelled.

Rando took snapshots of everything with his snap-shooter. Then he joined Thayla under the tree.

"See this?" he said as he brushed his hand against the grass. "Outside plants are green!"

Thayla didn't answer him. She was slowly waving her music gloves in the air. She was listening to her music while watching the gloves' colors sparkle in the sunlight.

Sunlight makes the colors brighter, Thayla thought. She was so happy with her music that she didn't notice the people who had gathered to watch her play. One man tossed a computer chip on the grass next to her. Another did the same, and then so did another.

A few people clapped when she stopped. Rando held up a chip. "I could get used to being an Outsider," he told Thayla. "Do you want something to eat? I'll go and buy us some Outsider food!"

Before Thayla could answer, Rando ran off. Soon he came back with two big sandwiches. Thayla had only seen people eat sandwiches in movies. From the looks on the people's faces, sandwiches didn't seem to taste very good. Thayla was so hungry that she would have eaten almost anything, though. She took off her gloves and put them in her pocket. When she took a bite from her sandwich, she was shocked at how tasty it was!

Both Rando and Thayla smiled as they ate their lunch. They learned that food could do more than just prevent them from starving. It could also taste great and be fun to eat.

After Rando finished eating, he wandered off to a store. Thayla looked around, smiling.

Then she caught sight of the big gray dome on the horizon. It made her nearly choke on her last bite of sandwich.

Thayla stood up and ran to the store where Rando was. She found him near a shelf of books and maps. "Hey, where do you want to go next?" he asked. "Landor is huge! Did you know that our planet has oceans?"

"Rando, we have to go back now."

Rando gave Thayla a strange look. "No way! There's a whole world out here!" he said.

"Yes, but our world is with the Insiders," said Thayla. She pointed to the gray dome in the distance. "If we don't go back, people will start asking questions. Our parents will get into big trouble. You know they will."

Rando looked at her and crossed his arms. "Can't you see? The dome is a joke," he said. "It's not fair that a few powerful people can keep the Insiders locked up. They're keeping us from the real world. All our lives we've been told that the Outsiders are sad and poor. The truth is, we're the ones who are sad and poor. Everything is better out here."

"I know, but we still have to go back, and you know that!" Thayla fired back. "How can we run away and leave everyone we love back inside the dome? Now let's go find a truck."

Rando frowned, but he followed Thayla as she left the store. Soon they saw an alley and ducked into it. A few seconds later, Thayla and Rando saw a floating truck turn into the alley. The truck headed straight toward a big metal box against a wall at the far end.

Rando looked around the alley. There were no guards in sight, so he ran to the box and quickly opened it. It was half empty, and there was enough room inside for Thayla and him.

"Come on," Rando whispered, pointing to the box. "Hurry up and get in. That truck will pick us up!"

CHAPTER 3
The Music Master

When the truck got back inside the dome, Thayla and Rando leaped out of the back. No guards saw them. They tiptoed behind a thick patch of trees on their way home.

Thayla was shaking. She was almost certain that they would get caught on the way back home. She had no idea what happened to Insiders caught going Outside, and she didn't want to find out.

"That was so easy!" Rando said. "Those guards at the gate are dumb!"

The guards are not dumb, Thayla thought. *They were just too tired to do their jobs well, like all Insiders!*

Suddenly, someone grabbed Rando and Thayla from behind. "Be quiet," a man's voice said. "You're coming with me!"

The two friends gasped and turned around quickly. They found themselves staring into the eyes of a smiling old man with a beard. It was Bombo, the music teacher!

Bombo lived in a small house in the woods at the edge of the city. Many young Insiders took music lessons from him. Their parents had learned to play their music gloves with Bombo when they were younger, too. Most Insiders gave up music as they got older, though.

Thayla and Rando soon found themselves sipping hot choco-milk in front of Bombo's fireplace. They were still shaking.

"You two seem pretty nervous," Bombo said. "Where have you been?"

Thayla and Rando looked at each other.

"Come on, you know you can tell me," Bombo said kindly.

Thayla couldn't lie to her old friend. She told him everything about their incredible day. Bombo rocked back and forth in his chair, thinking and listening.

"I had a feeling that you'd gone Outside," said Bombo after Thayla had finished her story. "Over the years I've seen many other young Insiders in the woods, going to and from the Outsiders' world."

Rando's jaw dropped. He almost spilled his choco-milk. "You mean others have done it, too? We thought we were the only ones!"

Bombo laughed. "I did it myself when I was a young one like you!"

"Then you know there's a better world out there!" cried Rando. "Why don't we all run away from this place?"

"You tell me," Bombo said. "Why did you come back?"

"This is the only life we know," Thayla replied sadly. "Yes, it's dreary and dull, but everyone we know lives here."

"Exactly," said Bombo, standing up. "The factory owners know that. They also know that most of us are not brave enough to escape. A few people get caught now and then, and they're never seen or heard from again. That's enough to keep most of us Inside."

Then Bombo's voice fell to a whisper. "We'll only be free if we all unite to bring down the dome. There's just one way to do it safely, but people are too scared to try."

"Tell us how!" Thayla cried.

"It's a pretty wild idea," Bombo sighed. "I don't think I could get enough people to try it with me." Bombo paused to look at his clock. "It's getting late," he said. "Your parents must be worried about you. You'd better get home."

Before Thayla left, she turned to Bombo. "Will you ever tell us how to bring down the dome?" she asked softly. 𝄿

Bombo gave her a solemn look. "I will when the time is right," he said. "I'll see you next week for your lesson. Keep playing your gloves, and remember that only music can make us happy."

The tele-visor played in the background while Thayla's family ate dinner in their kitchen. "It's Saturday night," the tele-visor said. "Have a happy and safe evening!"

Thayla looked at the screen and frowned. She couldn't keep her secret any longer. She took a deep breath and told her parents about what she had seen Outside. They were not pleased with her story.

"Do you know what happens to the parents of kids caught leaving the dome?" Thayla's mom asked. "We could lose our jobs, or worse! What were you thinking?"

"Let's just forget it ever happened," said Mr. Groono. He glared at Thayla.

Thayla nervously played with her hair, looking down. "I wasn't thinking," she said softly. "We really didn't mean to go Outside." Then her eyes grew wide. "You should have seen it out there, though. It was—"

"I don't want to hear another word, young lady!" said Mr. Groono. "Go to your room."

Thayla picked up her bowl of gray mush, ran to her room, and shut the door. Her heart sank. Her bed, her clothes, her books, and everything else looked so dreary.

From the family room, Thayla could hear a voice from the tele-visor say, "It's Saturday night. Have a happy and safe evening!" Thayla looked at her bowl of mush and sighed. *It's going to take time to get used to this again,* she thought. *Maybe I'll grow up to be just like Mom and Dad after all.* ⚡

CHAPTER 4
The Workers Unite

On Monday, Thayla noticed something very strange on her way to school. Someone had secretly put up posters on factory walls and shop windows all over the city. The posters had messages, such as "BETTER FOOD, BETTER PAY," "FEWER WORK HOURS," and "MORE TIME OFF." Guards were taking down the posters as quickly as they could, but there were lots of them.

Then Thayla stopped in her tracks. She stared at a giant snapshot pasted to a wall. The snapshot showed happy people walking down a pretty street lined with shops and trees. The scene looked familiar to her.

It's the street in the Outsider city! Thayla thought. She started running. She saw more huge snapshots pasted on walls. The snapshots showed Outsiders eating ice cream, and kids laughing. One showed a pretty park with the sun shining in the background.

At school, Thayla bumped into Rando. He looked scared. She grabbed his arm.

"Did you know your snapshots of the Outsiders are all over the city?" she asked.

"I know, I know!" whispered Rando. "I have no idea who posted them, though. The night we got back, my mom took all of the computer files out of the snap-shooter. She probably threw them away."

Thayla thought for a moment. Then her eyes lit up. "Maybe your mom copied the files before she threw them away!"

"I don't think my mom would do that. She believes in the dome," said Rando.

Suddenly a solemn voice came over a loudspeaker. "Attention, everyone! Dome guards are in the school checking the, uh, safety equipment. They say that we have to leave the building for a short time. We will have a time-out, starting now."

As everyone left for the time-out, Thayla saw that the guards were not checking safety equipment. Instead, they were tearing pictures of the Outside from the school walls.

"My mom is the only person I know who saw my snapshots," said Rando. "I'd better ask her what's going on."

"You know you can't see her now," Thayla said. "She's working at the factory!"

"I don't care! I have to get in to see her somehow," said Rando. Then he ran off.

Thayla sighed and caught up with him. As they ran through the streets of their city, the two friends passed more guards ripping down posters and pictures. Thayla and Rando finally reached the gates of the tall, gray factory where Rando's parents worked.

They stopped when they saw what was happening. A large crowd of workers stood outside the gates. Many of them were waving their pay envelopes.

"They took a chip from our pay just last week," cried one woman. "Another is missing this week. When will it end? We should all stop working. Then the factory will shut down, and the owners will have to listen to us."

"We have to work, though," said another worker. "We're lucky to have jobs at all. The Outsiders don't have it this good!"

"I'm sick of that lie!" one man said angrily. "Haven't you seen those pictures all over the city? The Outsiders have much better lives than we do! I'm not doing any more work until I get a better life, too." Other workers nodded, agreeing with him.

Thayla tugged at Rando's arm. "I don't like the look of this crowd. Maybe we should get back to school."

"I need to find my mom," Rando said. "I'm worried that someone will find out she had all those snapshots."

The factory whistle blew. "Attention, Insiders!" said a voice from a loudspeaker. "Kindly return to work. Kindly return to work. Kindly return . . . "

Nobody listened. A worker stood on a box and started shouting. She told the crowd to join people from other factories who were marching toward the main gates of the dome.

While most of the workers headed to the gates, some people started walking back toward the factories. Rando ran to one of them. It was his mom.

"Rando! Why are you and Thayla here?" asked Mrs. Nann with surprise. "You should be in school!"

"We have a time-out now," said Rando. "We have a question for you. Why are my pictures all over the city?"

Mrs. Nann looked nervous. "I kept all the files," she whispered. "The pictures looked so nice that I couldn't throw the files away."

"I knew it!" said Thayla with a big smile. "It was you who put up all the pictures. Now all of the Insiders can see what life is really like in the Outside world."

"I didn't put them up," said Mrs. Nann. "The next day I shared the files with my friends here at the factory. I didn't think they'd share the pictures with anyone else, but I was wrong."

Then Mrs. Nann looked down and sighed. "Sometimes a picture makes you see what you've been missing all your life." ⚡

"Hey, Mrs. Nann," one of the workers yelled. "Are you marching with us or not?"

Mrs. Nann didn't know what to say. She and the two young Insiders stood in the middle of the road. They watched as people walked past on their way to the gates.

Thayla smiled as she looked at the crowd of marchers. She had never seen the Insiders look so alive. She wondered about her own mom and dad. Were they going to the gates, too? There was only one way to find out.

Thayla tapped Mrs. Nann's shoulder. "Come on," she said. "Let's go to the gates. This is the day we've been waiting for."

CHAPTER 5

Inside Out

Thayla, Rando, and Mrs. Nann saw an incredible sight when they arrived at the main gates. A line of guards stood between the gates and a large crowd. The marchers couldn't get past the guards, so they were pounding on the dome wall instead.

Some people were busy pasting posters and Rando's snapshots onto the buildings closest to the dome. Others were shaking their fists at the trucks soaring above them. Thayla looked for her parents and soon found them. She was surprised to see her parents and neighbors putting up posters that read "BETTER FOOD, BETTER PAY."

A group of guards walked through the crowd, carrying chairs over their heads. They set up the chairs in front of the line of guards. Five people wearing business suits followed the guards and stood on the chairs.

"Attention, please," said one of the people who wore a suit. "The factory owners have asked us to come out to talk with you. We work for the

factories, too. We're here to help, so if you have a problem, write to us about it. Just drop a note in the factory suggestion boxes."

The workers in the crowd looked at each other. Then one woman shouted, "We don't want suggestion boxes—we want better pay!"

"We want better lives!" another worker called out.

"One at a time!" said a woman in a suit. She crossed her arms and gave the crowd a stern look. "This is not a good way to talk, so here's my suggestion. Go back to work. The factory owners will listen to you only after you've put your problems in writing."

The workers laughed at her. Thayla shouted something she had been thinking about for a long time. "Give us a door in the dome! We want doors so that we can see the Outside world for ourselves!"

"Doors! Doors! Yes! Give us doors!" the crowd shouted.

"Oh no, we mustn't have doors!" said one of the people in suits. "There's a lot of crime Outside. Harsh weather would come in. Doors would make the dome weak, too."

"What nonsense," said a voice from behind Thayla. She quickly turned around. Her music teacher was standing behind her.

"Bombo!" Thayla cried. "I'm so glad you came. Isn't this great? The factory owners just have to listen to us now. They have to give us what we want."

Bombo stroked his beard. "Is that so? What about giving ourselves what we want? Do you really think we need doors?"

Thayla gave him a stern look. "Of course we do!"

"Then why not make a door yourself right here?" he asked with a sly look on his face.

Bombo pulled on his music gloves. Pretty colors soon danced across his fingers, and soft music began to play. Then he rubbed his hands on the wall of the dome, playing music at the same time.

Thayla shook her head. *Bombo is nuts*, she thought. She noticed something very strange, though. As Bombo played his gloves, drops of water started falling from the dome above him.

Thayla looked up. The top of the dome was dripping with water. Bombo smiled. "See how the water falls? Our music can bring down the dome! Try it, Thayla. You've been practicing your music, haven't you?"

Thayla nodded. She pulled her bag off her shoulder and pulled her gloves out. She put them on and rubbed them against the wall. Thayla felt the wall shake. More water dripped from above.

Thayla looked over at Rando and his mom. "Come on, get out your gloves and play some music!" Thayla shouted with joy.

Mrs. Nann rubbed her chin and stared. "Why, I haven't played those things in years," she said. "Do you have your gloves, son?"

Rando dug through his bag. "Sure I do!" He pulled out his own gloves and put them on.

Word spread quickly. Every Insider with a pair of music gloves ran to find a place at the dome wall. Eight gloves against the dome wall became 16, then 32, then 64, and so on.

It was the most wonderful sound that Thayla had ever heard. The gloves played the music of every Insider's heart. There were songs of hope, songs of love, and songs of dreams. When all the songs came together, the sound was beautiful.

The people in business suits screamed at the crowd. "Stop! You don't know what you're doing! There is nothing in the Outside world you want to see! Guards, stop them!"

Their cries were useless. In fact, some of the guards put on music gloves, too. Soon everyone in the crowd was either playing music or cheering loudly.

A noise like thunder came from the top of the dome. The ceiling seemed to open up. Then a soft, misty rain began to fall.

"It's beautiful!" cried Mrs. Groono, who had come to stand beside Thayla.

Thayla closed her eyes and took a deep breath. The air was no longer stuffy. Instead, she smelled the fresh scent of real flowers and grass. It was the same sweet scent she had smelled in the park Outside.

Bombo backed away from the dome wall and shook his head. His hair and beard were

wet from the falling water. "I never thought I would live to see this day," he said.

"You did it!" Rando yelled, pumping his fist in the air.

"You mean *we* did it!" Bombo shouted.

Thayla just smiled. She looked up and kept rubbing her hands against the dome wall. Drops of rain settled on her hair like jewels.

Then a large piece of the dome wall melted away in front of Thayla. It left behind a large hole. Thayla stared at the hole.

Bombo put his hand on her shoulder. "Go ahead," he whispered. "You can be the first."

Thayla paused for a moment. She felt her heart trembling. Then she stepped slowly through the hole and into the warmth of a new day. It was sunny Outside. ⚡